Whole Body Listening Larry at Home!

2nd Edition

Kristen Wilson & Elizabeth Sautter

Illustrated by Eric Hutchison

! Social Thinking®

Whole Body Listening Larry at Home! 2nd Edition

Kristen Wilson and Elizabeth Sautter

Illustrations by Eric Hutchison, ehutch5@gmail.com

Edited by Ann L. Pendley, Ph.D., CCC-SLP

ISBN: 978-1-936943-31-9

Think Social Publishing, Inc.
404 Saratoga Avenue
Santa Clara, CA 95050
Tel: (408) 557-8595
Fax: (408) 557-8594

This book was printed and bound in the United States by Mighty Color Printing.

TSP is a sole source provider of Social Thinking products in the U.S.

Books may be purchased online at www.socialthinking.com

Thank you to:

Susanne Poulette Truesdale for originating the concept of whole body listening.

To Michelle Garcia Winner for her work and inspiration in the area of Social Thinking.

And to the amazing therapists and clients with whom we work at Communication Works in Oakland, CA; they inspire us everyday.

What is Whole Body Listening?

Whole body listening is more than just "hearing" with the ears. It includes:

- listening with the eyes - looking toward the speaker

- listening with the ears – both ears ready to hear

- listening with the mouth – quiet and waiting for your turn to talk

- listening with the body – facing toward speaker

- listening with the hands – quiet and kept to yourself

- listening with the feet – quiet and still

- listening with the brain – thinking about what is being said

- listening with the heart – considering the speaker and others listening

As adults we often forget to talk about what listening means and what it looks like in our conversations with young learners. How often do you find yourself using phrases with your child such as, "pay attention" or "listen carefully" at the dinner table or when company is over? When we make these requests, we don't really realize that along with what we're saying comes the unspoken expectation that we want them to also stop whatever they are doing and show us they are listening. That means their whole body is engaged (they look at us, keep still, think about what we said, etc.). However, do we ever really say that or teach that to them? And, then what happens when the child doesn't show those behaviors? We feel frustrated and assume they aren't listening, don't want to comply, etc.

As parents, grandparents, or caregivers, we need to understand that "listening" is an abstract concept, one that involves a complex set of skills for a child. It involves integrating all of the body senses (sensory processing), combining that with self control of our brain and body (executive functioning) and thinking of others and what they are saying and why (perspective taking).

This is not an easy task to execute. Many children do not fully understand what is expected of them when we ask them to listen and some children may not be able to physically or cognitively meet the expected behaviors that are involved.

To make this abstract skill more concrete, in 1990 speech pathologist Susanne Poulette Truesdale created the concept "whole body listening" to explain how each body part is involved. Other professionals have expanded the initial whole body listening concept to include the heart as a way to encourage empathy and perspective taking. This later addition is helpful when children are working on social interactions and relationships. When we are around other people the purpose of listening is not just to "hear" and interpret what is being said, but also to demonstrate shared involvement and to make a positive impression.

This expanded concept of whole body listening is woven into parts of Michelle Garcia Winner's larger Social Thinking® methodology to teach the fundamentals of how and why we listen to figure out the "expected" behavior when around others. Similar to other Social Thinking Vocabulary that breaks down the social code, whole body listening has become a foundational concept to help make this and other abstract concepts more concrete and easier to understand, teach and practice.

Truesdale emphasizes that whole body listening is "a tool, not a rule," meaning that adults need to think flexibly about how best to use it. There is no "one way" to teach the whole body listening concept and there is no "one way" for children to demonstrate it. The goal when teaching this concept is to create effective approaches for those with a variety of learning styles. And most importantly, to do this in ways that respect each person's particular needs and abilities. For instance, one child may have sensory issues that make it difficult for him to look and listen at the same time. Another child may not yet understand the use of body language and that people consider both her words and her actions when figuring out meaning in a social situation. She may be saying "I'm listening" but her body language may be sending a different message. Our kids with learning differences, and even those without, may need adaptations or modifications made for them to feel and be successful demonstrating whole body listening. For more information on adapting the concept to different learners, please refer to the article, "Taking a Deeper Look at Whole Body Listening" (Sautter, 2015) found at www.socialthinking.com.

The book, *Whole Body Listening Larry at Home*, was developed to give families and caregivers a tool to teach and talk about the complex concept of listening, an important "readiness" skill. It helps children understand the importance of attending and being part of a group. Paying attention and listening to others (adults, teachers, peers, etc.) are not only considered essential for social communication and social success, but are also fundamental abilities for learning to be part of a group and for academic success. In fact, these skills are clearly outlined in the Common Core and State Standards that teachers use to grade their students. They are also key components to schoolwide initiatives for PBIS (Positive Behavioral Interventions and Supports) that aim to create a positive and caring school culture among children, and for successful social emotional learning (SEL) skills. When an abstract concept such as listening is broken down and explained in a concrete, structured, and systematic manner, parents are equipped with the tools to make this learning come alive for their children right from the start. The goal of this book (and its companion book, *Whole Body Listening Larry at School*) is to do just that.

How to Use this Book and Encourage Discussion

The following are suggestions for parents and caregivers to consider while reading the book and to use at other times during the many natural teachable moments that arise throughout the day. These suggestions can be used with children with and without social challenges, including those with ADHD, ASD (Level 1 and 2), hyperlexia, gifted and talented/2E, social communication disorders, etc. We encourage you to modify any of these suggestions and create new strategies to use with your children that support their particular needs. Remember to consider each child's developmental and cognitive ability.

As you read the story:
• Take time to look at and talk about all the pictures in the book with your child. Make note of the characters' facial expressions, body positioning, thoughts and feelings. Discuss what it means to listen with each body part.

• As you move through the storybook, have your child point out and discuss the body parts that are active and not active during whole body listening in each particular situation.

• Talk about how the characters in the book feel when they are not listening or being listened to and why they feel this way. Ask your child to imagine how he or she would feel in similar situations. Be sure to explore listening from all angles: the child being listened to and not being listened to as well as the child listening/not listening to others. For instance: "How did Grandma feel when you were using whole body listening while she talked about her vacation?" Some children may get frustrated when they are not being listened to, but don't realize when they themselves are not listening and are creating that same feeling in others.

· Discuss whole body listening with the entire family. Discuss how whole body listening applies to situations at home and settings beyond the home such as the playground, school, birthday parties, etc. Have the entire family brainstorm together what behavior is expected for various events and family situations.

· Discuss what it means to self-advocate when listening is difficult or becomes difficult for a child. Be proactive and give your children phrases to use when they get to this point. For instance: "Can I take a short break?", "It's really hard for me to listen with my eyes while at the dinner table" or "It's getting hard for me to keep my hands quiet while we watch the movie. Is it okay to get my squishy ball to play with for the rest of the movie?"

Please refer to the end of the book for functional ways to teach and use the concept of whole body listening along with suggestions for accommodations to consider for individuals who struggle with this concept.

Everyday when Larry comes home from school he sits at the kitchen table and shares a jelly sandwich with his mom. They talk about his fun day at school.

I played tag with Liam at recess!

It is nice talking with Larry when he is listening with his whole body.

1

"Sister Lucy," Larry says,
"people don't know you are listening when you look to the skies.
When you think about others, try to listen with your eyes!"

4

"Sister Lucy," Larry says, "with all that banging, we can't hear Mom's plans. Put down that fork and listen with your hands!"

"Sister Lucy," Larry says, "you're making so much noise, kicking Dad's seat!
Let your legs relax and listen with your feet."

"Sister Lucy," Larry says, "Dad is getting more upset each time he appears, put that game on hold and listen with your ears."

9

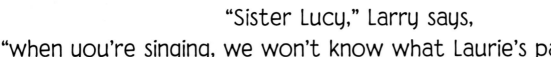

"Sister Lucy," Larry says,
"when you're singing, we won't know what Laurie's party is about.
When others are talking try to listen with your mouth."

"Sister Lucy," Larry says,
"for Grandma to have comfortable thoughts about you,
please let me explain — ignore the TV, and listen with your brain!"

"Sister Lucy," Larry says, "Laurie is excited and YOU talk about your art. She is sharing something special; please listen with your heart!"

15

"Sister Lucy," Larry says,
"Grandpa's feeling frustrated – there is so much that you're missin'.
Stop all that wiggling and let your body listen."

17

"Oh my!" Lucy exclaims, "Larry has taught me so much about how to listen with my eyes, ears, hands, feet, heart, body, and brain! My unexpected behavior put my family to the test, but Larry showed me that whole body listening is the best!"

21

"Sister Lucy," Larry says,
"look at everyone's face – so many positive thoughts are happening because you are using whole body listening!"

How to Teach and Implement Whole Body Listening at Home

The following activities help parents and caregivers introduce and reinforce teaching the whole body listening concept. As with other tools and materials, the abilities and developmental level of each individual must be considered. Some of the skills used in whole body listening, such as maintaining eye contact, keeping one's body parts still, or remaining quiet, are extremely difficult and may cause stress or simply not be possible for certain people at certain times. When this is the case it's important that adults demonstrate awareness and understanding and make any needed modifications to help the child be successful in learning to listen and be part of a group.

For early learners:

· Make a copy of Larry and the body parts (eyes, ears, mouth, hands, feet, body, brain, and heart) from page 27 of the book. This same coloring page is available as a free download at this book's product page at www.socialthinking.com. Have your child cut these out and then use them while discussing how each body part contributes to whole body listening. These can also be cut out from felt and used on a felt board.

· Using the figure of Larry, ask your child to circle the body parts involved in whole body listening as you go through each one.

· Use a potato head figure to demonstrate and discuss whole body listening. Put the pieces of the body together. A hat can be used to represent the brain and a heart-shaped paper cutout to represent the heart. Have your child talk about how each part contributes to whole body listening.

· Sing the song "Head, shoulders, knees and toes ...," but substitute the lyrics with body parts for whole body listening (eyes, ears, mouth and hands, mouth and hands...).

· Play Simon Says and have your child start by showing a wiggly, noisy body and then have the child follow what "Simon Says" by listening with the various body parts. For instance, "Simon says, listen with your feet."

· Read books that show the characters using or not using whole body listening. Two suggestions include *Howard B. Wigglebottom Learns to Listen* by Howard Binkow, and *Five Little Monkeys Jumping on the Bed* by Eileen Christelow. Have your child identify how the characters are or are not listening with their whole body.

For elementary grade children and up:

• Provide visuals such as drawings or photos of various situations (e.g., at the dinner table, watching a movie, etc.) to give your child a mental image and provide situational awareness for these contexts and expectations. The visuals in the book can be used for this as well. For more information on this idea, see the article "Using Whole Body Listening to Increase Executive Functioning" by Elizabeth Sautter and Sarah Ward (2013).

• Act out and role-play expected listening behavior in a given scenario, such as working in a small group. This provides more structure and a mental screenplay for children to practice within.

• To teach self-awareness, photocopy the body parts involved in whole body listening and paste them on a poster board for your child to view. Talk about what comes easy for them, and which parts of whole body listening are more challenging. Next, take a photo of your child using whole body listening and paste that to the poster as well. Place the poster on the refrigerator or their bedroom door. Refer to it during teachable moments throughout the day.

• Watch television shows or cartoons and discuss whether or not the characters are listening with their whole body and how the others characters feel when this happens.

• Record a video of your child in a situation where he or she is using (or should be using) whole body listening. Review the clip together and discuss the child's behavior.

• If you have more than one child, or a group is playing together, present a list of available group games. Once kids have decided which one to play, have them practice using whole body listening during the game. Not all body parts are expected to be quiet or still while playing games (i.e., it's okay to move around during some games). Discuss their thoughts and feelings about how this activity went for the group.

How to Encourage Whole Body Listening Across the Day

• Incorporate the whole body listening vocabulary into daily routines and make it a common language used at home with your family and other people who spend time with your child (grandparents, baby sitters, teachers, therapists, etc.).

- Review expected listening behavior for your child prior to each listening situation. When more intense, focused listening is expected for an activity (e.g., reading or dinner time) review all eight parts of whole body listening. Remind your child what each one looks like and why each one is important to the situation.

- Before going into a social situation, prime, prepare and plan to set your child up for success. Discuss the hidden rules and expected behavior in the situation. For instance, "At the movie theatre we listen with our feet and don't kick the seat in front of us."

- Once your child has a solid understanding of whole body listening, before entering a new or different situation, tell the child that "sometime soon" or "in the next hour" he or she will have the opportunity to practice whole body listening. This primes the child's awareness ahead of time and provides an opportunity to practice using the concept independently.

- Praise/acknowledge children when they are using whole body listening, being aware of their body, using a tool and/or advocating for themselves. For example, "I see that you are listening with your hands," or "I like how you're trying to use your brain to think about what I'm saying."

- Consider introducing mindfulness (being aware of the present moment), breathing exercises or other relaxation strategies to increase the mind-body connection and awareness.

References

Binkow, H. (2006). *Howard B. Wigglebottom Learns to Listen*. Minneapolis, MN: Lerner Publishing Group.

Christelow, E. (1989). *Five Little Monkeys Jumping on the Bed*. New York, NY: Clarion Books.

Sautter, E. (2015). "Taking a Deeper Look at Whole Body Listening." Social Thinking Publishing Newsletter, October 2015.

Sautter, E. and Kuypers, L. (2012). "Promoting Social Regulation." *Autism Bay Area*, May-June 2012.

Sautter, E. and Ward, S. (2013). "Using Whole Body Listening to Increase Executive Functioning Skills." *Autism Bay Area*, January-Febuary 2013.

Truesdale, S.P. (2013). "Whole Body Listening Updated." Advance for Speech-LanguagePathologists & Audiologists, Volume 23, No. 3, 8-10. Available online at: http://speech-language-pathology-audiology.advanceweb.com/Features/Articles/Whole-Body-Listening-Updated.aspx

Truesdale, S. P. (1990). "Whole-Body Listening: Developing Active Auditory Skills". *Language, Speech, and Hearing Services in Schools*, Volume 21, July 1990, 183-184.

Handout for Whole Body Listening

Eyes – looking toward the speaker

Ears – ready to hear

Mouth – quiet and waiting for your turn to talk

Hands – quiet and kept to yourself

Feet – quiet and still

Body – facing toward the speaker

Brain – thinking about what is being said

Heart – considering the speaker and others listening

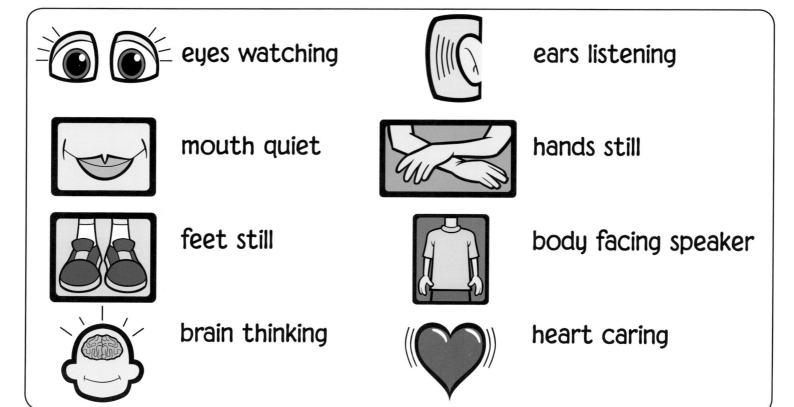

eyes watching

ears listening

mouth quiet

hands still

feet still

body facing speaker

brain thinking

heart caring

SocialThinking® has so much to offer!

OUR MISSION

At Social Thinking, our mission is to help people develop social competencies to better connect with others and experience deeper well-being. We create unique treatment frameworks and strategies to help individuals develop their social thinking and related social skills to meet their academic, personal and professional social goals. These goals often include sharing space effectively with others, learning to work as part of a team, and developing relationships of all kinds: with family, friends, classmates, co-workers, romantic partners, etc.

ARTICLES

100+ free educational articles and treatment strategies

CONFERENCES, eLEARNING & CUSTOM TRAINING

Courses and embedded training for schools and organizations

PRODUCTS

Books, games, posters, music and more!

CLINICAL RESEARCH

Measuring the effectiveness of the Social Thinking Methodology

TREATMENT: CHILDREN & ADULTS

Clinical treatment, assessments, school consultations, etc.

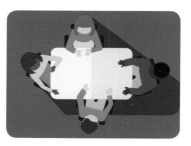

CLINICAL TRAINING PROGRAM

Three-day intensive training for professionals